W9-BOB-343
NORMAL PUBLIC LIBRARY
A12004 556793

HORSES

The Shetland Pony

by Amanda Parise-Peterson

Consultant:
Elaine Ward
Shetland Pony Stud-Book Society (SPSBS)
Perth, Scotland

Capstone
press

Mankato, Minnesota

Edge Books are published by Capstone Press,
151 Good Counsel Drive, P.O. Box 669, Mankato, Minnesota 56002.
www.capstonepress.com

Printed in the United States of America

Library of Congress Cataloging-in-Publication Data
Parise-Peterson, Amanda.
The Shetland pony / by Amanda Parise-Peterson.
p. cm.—(Edge Books. Horses.)
Summary: "Describes the Shetland Pony, including its history, physical features, and uses today"—Provided by publisher.
Includes bibliographical references and index.
ISBN 0-7368-4374-4 (hardcover)
1. Shetland pony—Juvenile literature. I. Title. II. Series.
SF315.2.S5P27 2006
636.1'6—dc22 2004030235

Editorial Credits
Carrie A. Braulick, editor; Juliette Peters, designer; Deirdre Barton, photo researcher/photo editor

Photo Credits
Alan Spencer, cover
Capstone Press/Gary Sundermeyer 6; Karon Dubke, 20
Corbis/Kevin Schafer, 5; Kit Houghton, 26
Courtesy of the Personal Ponies Organization, 27
June Brown, 13, 14, 19, 25
Karen Patterson, 12
Mane Photo/Jennay Hilesman, 11
© 2004 Mark J. Barrett, back cover, 16–17, 29
Marvin Subbert (owner)/Van Meer (photographer), 22
Shetland Museum, 7
Valerie Russell, 21
Zona Schneider, 8

Capstone Press thanks staff of the American Shetland Pony Club for their assistance in preparing this book.

1 2 3 4 5 6 10 09 08 07 06 05

Table of Contents

FEATURES

Chapter 1

Hard Times

Shetland ponies are small. Many fully grown Shetlands only reach to the waist of an average-sized adult. But Shetlands are one of the strongest horse breeds for their size. Long ago, people used the ponies to pull wagons loaded with supplies. Today, Shetlands are popular children's ponies.

On the Islands

Shetland ponies receive their name from the Shetland Islands north of Scotland. Ponies have lived on the Shetland Islands for at least 2,000 years. Nobody knows for certain how the ponies got to the islands.

Learn about:

- Early uses
- Jack 16
- Shetland registries

Today, about 1,000 Shetland ponies live on the Shetland Islands.

By the 1600s, people living on the islands used the ponies for work. The ponies hauled farm supplies and a material called peat. The islanders used peat to heat their homes.

A New Job

In 1842, a change in one of Great Britain's laws made work a way of life for many Shetland ponies. This law banned young children from working in coal mines. Mine owners then began using ponies in mines. They liked Shetlands because the ponies fit into the small spaces of mines. The strong ponies also could pull heavy wagons loaded with coal.

People living on the Shetland Islands shipped thousands of ponies to Great Britain for mining. Most of these "pit ponies" were only let out of the dark, dirty mines once each year. By the late 1800s, the islands' population of Shetlands had dropped from 10,000 to 5,000.

FACT

In the 1600s, people on the Shetland Islands used hair from the manes and tails of Shetland ponies to make fishing line.

Hauling peat was one of the first uses for Shetland ponies.

Breeding Shetlands

Mine owners chose strong Shetlands to work in their mines. Weaker ponies were left behind on the islands. Mine owner Lord Londonderry wanted a better supply of suitable mining ponies. In 1870, he set up a breeding farm on the islands. His stallion Jack 16 became an important ancestor of today's Shetlands.

Modern American Shetlands have slender necks and legs.

Shetlands in the United States

People first brought Shetlands to the United States in the 1880s. Soon, people began to breed the ponies. Some breeders wanted ponies with an elegant look. They bred tall, slender Shetlands. Over time, they created ponies that were less muscular than those from the Shetland Islands. These ponies became known as classic American Shetlands.

People in the United States also bred Shetlands with Hackney ponies. The breeding produced lively, high-stepping ponies. Today, these ponies are called modern American Shetlands.

Shetland Registries

In 1888, U.S. Shetland owners formed the American Shetland Pony Club (ASPC). The club kept track of each registered Shetland's ancestry. Since it began, the ASPC has registered about 150,000 ponies.

In 1890, British Shetland pony owners formed the Shetland Pony Stud-Book Society (SPSBS). They registered about 500 ponies. Today, the SPSBS registers Shetlands that are descendants of these ponies. It registers about 2,500 foals each year.

Tough and Tender

Over hundreds of years, ponies of the Shetland Islands developed features to handle their living conditions. The ponies' small size helped them survive on little food. They grew long coats and manes to stay warm during cold winters.

Most modern Shetlands no longer face hard living conditions. But they still share many features of their ancestors.

Size

Shetland ponies are measured from the ground to the highest point of their shoulders, or withers. They are measured in inches.

Learn about:

- ★ Miniature Shetlands
- ★ Colors
- ★ Guard hairs

Many of today's Shetlands live in large, grassy pastures.

Shetland ponies have wide foreheads and small ears.

Most Shetlands are between 27 and 42 inches (69 and 107 centimeters) tall. The SPSBS registers only ponies that are 42 inches tall or less at age 4 or older. The ASPC allows Shetlands to be as tall as 46 inches (117 centimeters).

The smallest Shetlands are called miniature Shetlands. These ponies are 34 inches (86 centimeters) tall or less at age 4 or older.

Build and Color

Small size is just one feature that Shetlands share. Shetlands have rounded bodies and muscular hindquarters. They have short legs and tough, round hooves. Their sloped shoulders lead to a muscular neck. Shetlands have small heads with wide foreheads. They have small ears and large nostrils.

Shetlands can be almost any color. Colors include black, chestnut, gray, bay, and piebald. Chestnut is a copper color. Bay ponies are a shade of brown. They have black manes and tails. Bay ponies also have black coloring on their lower legs. Piebald ponies have black and white patches.

Bay Shetland ponies have black manes and tails.

Warm Coats

Unlike other horses, Shetland ponies grow double coats in winter. The inside coat is soft. The outer coat is thick. Long hairs called guard hairs keep water from reaching the inside layer. The coat is so protective that snow often lies unmelted on a Shetland's back.

Double coats keep snow from melting on the backs of Shetland ponies.

FACT
Like the Shetland pony, other animals from the Shetland Islands are small with thick coats. These animals include Shetland sheepdogs and Shetland sheep.

Personality

Shetland ponies are gentle. They bond strongly with their owners and handlers. These features make them good ponies for children. Managers of riding programs for children with disabilities often use Shetlands.

The intelligence of Shetland ponies helps them learn quickly. Some Shetlands learn tricks that they perform in circuses. They may learn to rear, walk on their hind legs, or perform with other animals.

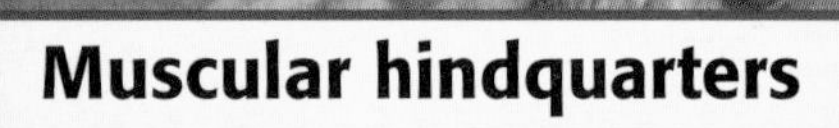
Muscular hindquarters
Short legs

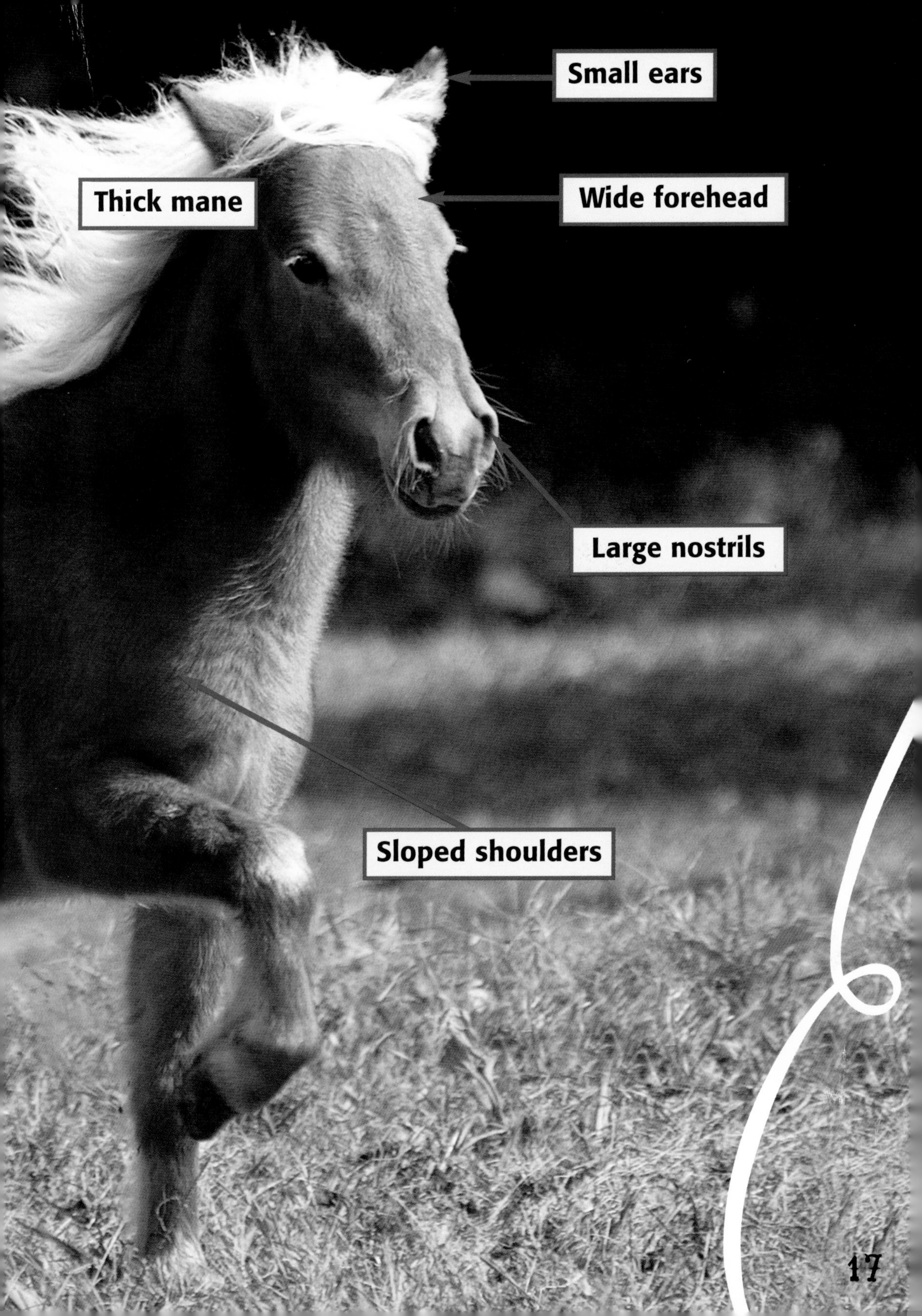

Small ears

Thick mane

Wide forehead

Large nostrils

Sloped shoulders

Chapter 3

A Show Pony for Everyone

By the 1950s, machines had replaced Shetland ponies in coal mines. People then kept Shetlands as pets and as children's ponies. Some owners competed with their ponies at shows. Shetlands were strong competitors against larger horse breeds. Today, the ponies compete at all-Shetland events and at shows with other breeds.

Learn about:

- **Shows in the United Kingdom**
- **ASPC show classes**
- **Shetland Congress**

Shetlands are popular show ponies for children.

Performance Award Scheme

The United Kingdom is home to many all-Shetland competitions. The most popular events are part of the Performance Award Scheme. Members of the SPSBS started the scheme in 1980. Riders 14 years old or younger compete in the scheme.

Scheme events include lead rein, dressage, and gymkhana. In lead rein, a handler leads a pony while a young child rides it. Riders competing in dressage guide their ponies through a series of advanced moves. Ponies may step sideways or turn while keeping their front legs in place. Gymkhana is a combination of games that test the skills of ponies and riders. Gymkhana ponies must be fast and easy to control.

Riders earn points at each Performance Award Scheme event. At the end of the season, the rider with the most points receives the Nan French trophy.

Shetland Pony Grand National

Some riders in the Performance Award Scheme also compete in the Shetland Pony Grand National. This event is held each December during the Olympia International Horse Show in London, England. It is based on the famous Grand National race for adult riders.

At the Shetland Grand National, riders jump over brush fences that are about 2 feet (.6 meter) high. The rider who completes the jumps the fastest wins.

The Shetland Grand National raises money for children's charities. The event has raised more than $250,000 since it started in 1982.

Shows in the United States

The American Shetland Pony Club sets up rules for most Shetland shows in the United States. Ponies that participate in these shows must be registered by the ASPC.

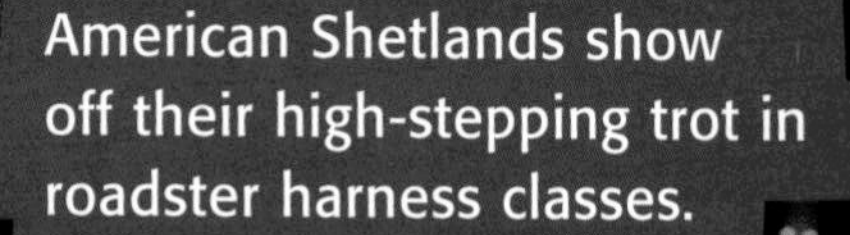

American Shetlands show off their high-stepping trot in roadster harness classes.

FACT
Curtiss-Frisco Pete is one of the most famous modern American Shetlands. He received the title of national champion stallion in the halter class six times.

Most shows include halter, riding, and harness classes. In halter classes, handlers lead their ponies around the ring. Judges score the ponies on their physical features. Ponies pull carts in harness classes.

Each year, the ASPC holds the Shetland Congress. Ponies that win at the show receive national champion titles. In 2004, about 500 ponies competed at the Shetland Congress. The number of entries set a show record.

Training Shetlands

People train Shetland ponies much like they train larger horses. Many Shetland breeders begin handling a foal right after it is born. After a few months, trainers fit a halter around a pony's head. They teach the pony to lead. By age 4, Shetlands usually are strong enough to be ridden.

Chapter 4

Shetlands in Action

Shetlands are competitive at events other than shows. In the midwestern United States, people compete with their Shetlands in pulling contests. Ponies that pull the heaviest loads win the events.

Strong legs give Shetland ponies good jumping abilities. Some Shetlands jump at the U.S. Equestrian National Pony Hunter Championships that are held each year.

Learn about:

- **Pulling contests**
- **Shetlands in jumping events**
- **Caring for Shetlands**

Some people compete with their Shetlands in jumping events.

Most Shetlands need only pasture grass to eat.

Care

Caring for Shetlands is slightly different from taking care of other horses. Shetland ponies are hardy. They can handle cold weather better than other horses can.

Shetlands rarely need as much food as other ponies. Many people feed ponies both hay and grain. Shetlands usually need only pasture grass or hay. Shetlands that eat too much can develop a foot disease called laminitis.

Shetlands have tough feet. But they still need their hooves trimmed regularly. Some ponies wear shoes to protect their feet.

Shetland owners throughout the world treasure their strong, talented ponies. Shetlands are sure to remain one of the world's most popular pony breeds in the future.

Personal Ponies

In 1986, Marianne Alexander formed an organization called Personal Ponies. She brought Shetlands from the United Kingdom to the United States. She gave the ponies to children with disabilities. Today, Personal Ponies has grown. About 50 farms throughout the United States breed Shetlands for the organization. Personal Ponies provides hundreds of ponies to children each year.

Fast Facts:
The Shetland Pony

Name: Shetland ponies are named for the Shetland Islands.

History: Shetland ponies have lived on the Shetland Islands for thousands of years. In the 1800s, people shipped many Shetlands to Great Britain and the United States.

Height: Shetland ponies usually stand between 27 and 42 inches (69 and 107 centimeters) tall at the withers. Some American Shetlands are as tall as 46 inches (117 centimeters).

Weight: Shetland ponies usually weigh between 300 and 450 pounds (140 and 200 kilograms).

Colors: Shetlands can be almost any color. Common colors are black, chestnut, gray, bay, and brown.

Features: small head; small ears; wide forehead; thick mane; large nostrils; rounded body; strong hindquarters; thick, double winter coats; tough hooves

Personality: gentle, intelligent, independent

Abilities: Shetlands compete at shows in harness, riding, and halter classes. They also have good jumping abilities.

Life span: about 20 to 25 years

Glossary

ancestor (AN-sess-tur)—a member of a breed that lived a long time ago

dressage (druh-SAHJ)—a riding style in which horses complete a pattern while doing advanced moves

foal (FOHL)—a horse that is less than 1 year old

gymkhana (jim-KHA-nuh)—a combination of competitive games on horseback

halter (HAWL-tur)—a rope or strap used to lead a horse; the halter fits over the horse's nose and behind its ears.

harness (HAR-niss)—a set of leather straps and metal pieces that connect a horse to a cart

laminitis (lah-muh-NYE-tuhss)—a painful hoof disease of horses

peat (PEET)—dark brown, partly decayed plant matter that is found in bogs and swamps; peat can be used as fuel.

registry (REH-juh-stree)—an organization that keeps track of the ancestry for horses of a certain breed

stallion (STAL-yuhn)—an adult male horse that can be used for breeding

Read More

Barnes, Julia. *101 Facts about Horses and Ponies.* 101 Facts about Pets. Milwaukee: Gareth Stevens, 2002.

Lomberg, Michelle. *Caring for Your Horse.* Caring for Your Pet. New York: Weigl Publishers, 2004.

Ransford, Sandy. *Horse and Pony Breeds.* Kingfisher Riding Club. Boston: Kingfisher, 2003.

Internet Sites

FactHound offers a safe, fun way to find Internet sites related to this book. All of the sites on FactHound have been researched by our staff.

Here's how:

1. Visit *www.facthound.com*
2. Type in this special code **0736843744** for age-appropriate sites. Or enter a search word related to this book for a more general search.
3. Click on the **Fetch It** button.

FactHound will fetch the best sites for you!

Index